For Abigail, Henry, David and Cat – K.F.

To A, your constant support is what keeps me going – A.C.

First published in Great Britain 2026 by Red Shed, part of Farshore
An imprint of HarperCollins*Publishers*
1 London Bridge Street, London SE1 9GF
www.farshore.co.uk

HarperCollins*Publishers*
Macken House, 39/40 Mayor Street Upper,
Dublin 1, D01 C9W8, Ireland

Red Shed is a registered trademark of HarperCollins*Publishers* Ltd.

Text © HarperCollins*Publishers* 2026
Illustrations © Aaron Cushley 2026
Aaron Cushley has asserted his moral rights.

Consultancy by Professor Julie Anderson, Professor Caroline Archer-Parré, Lara Bampfield, Professor Paul Barrett, Dr Mehreen Chida-Razvi, Ilia Curto Pelle, Professor Emeritus Colin Divall, Dr Jane Draycott, Dr Alex Fitzpatrick, Dr Elizabeth Frood, Professor Alexander Geurds, Dr Neil Handley, Professor Mike Parker Pearson, Professor Martin Polley, Professor Katie Sampeck.

ISBN 978 0 00 876504 0
Printed and bound in Malaysia.
1

A CIP catalogue record for this title is available from the British Library.

All rights reserved. No part of this publication may be reproduced, stored in a retrieval system, or transmitted, in any form or by any means, electronic, mechanical, photocopying, recording or otherwise, without the prior permission of the publisher and copyright owner.

Without limiting the exclusive rights of any author, contributor or the publisher of this publication, any unauthorised use of this publication to train generative artificial intelligence (AI) technologies is expressly prohibited. HarperCollins also exercise their rights under Article 4(3) of the Digital Single Market Directive 2019/790 and expressly reserve this publication from the text and data mining exception.

Stay safe online. Any website addresses listed in this book are correct at the time of going to print. However, Farshore is not responsible for content hosted by third parties. Please be aware that online content can be subject to change and websites can contain content that is unsuitable for children. We advise that all children are supervised when using the internet.

MIX
Paper | Supporting responsible forestry
FSC® C007207

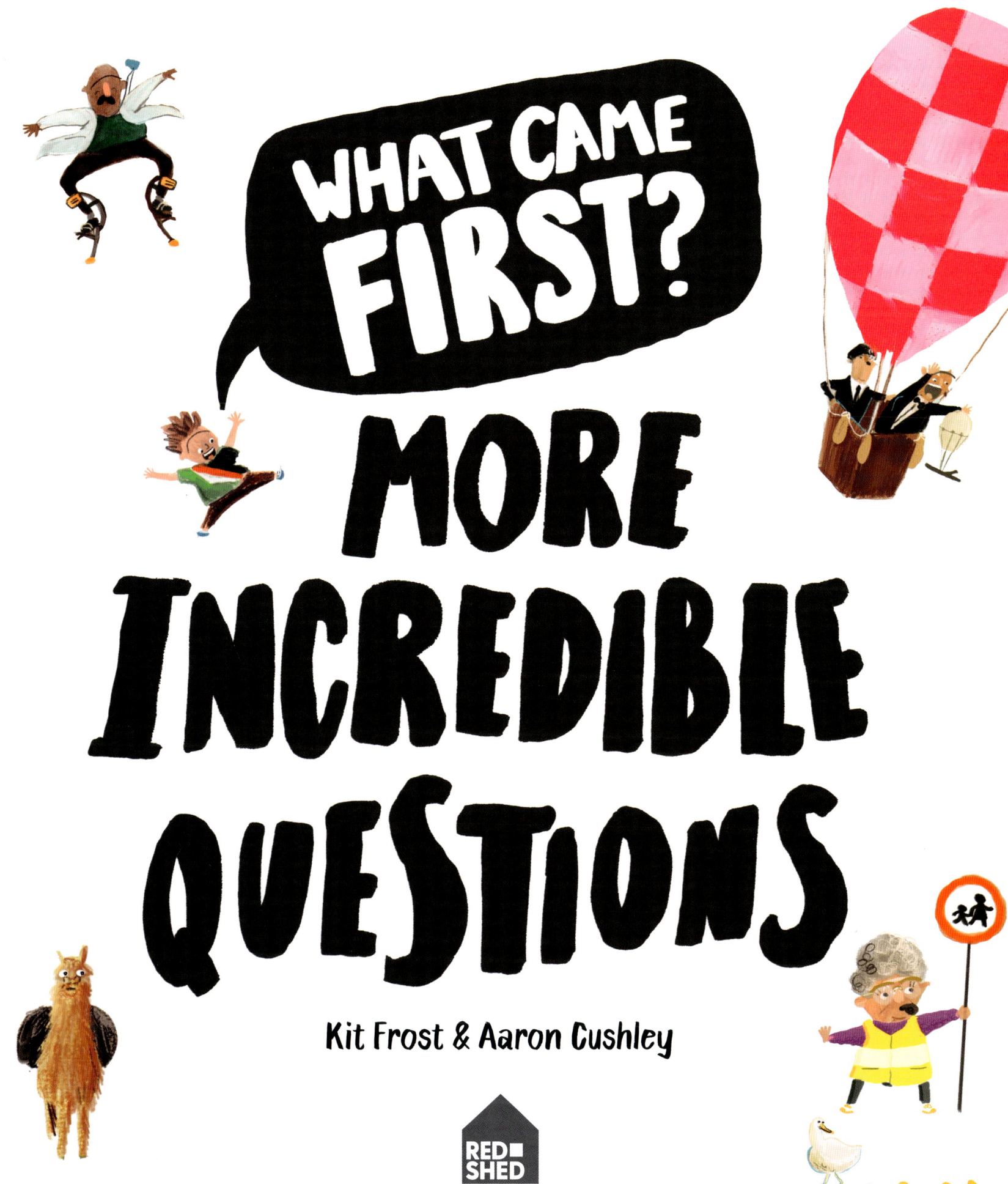
WHAT CAME FIRST?

MORE INCREDIBLE QUESTIONS

Kit Frost & Aaron Cushley

RED SHED

INTRODUCTION

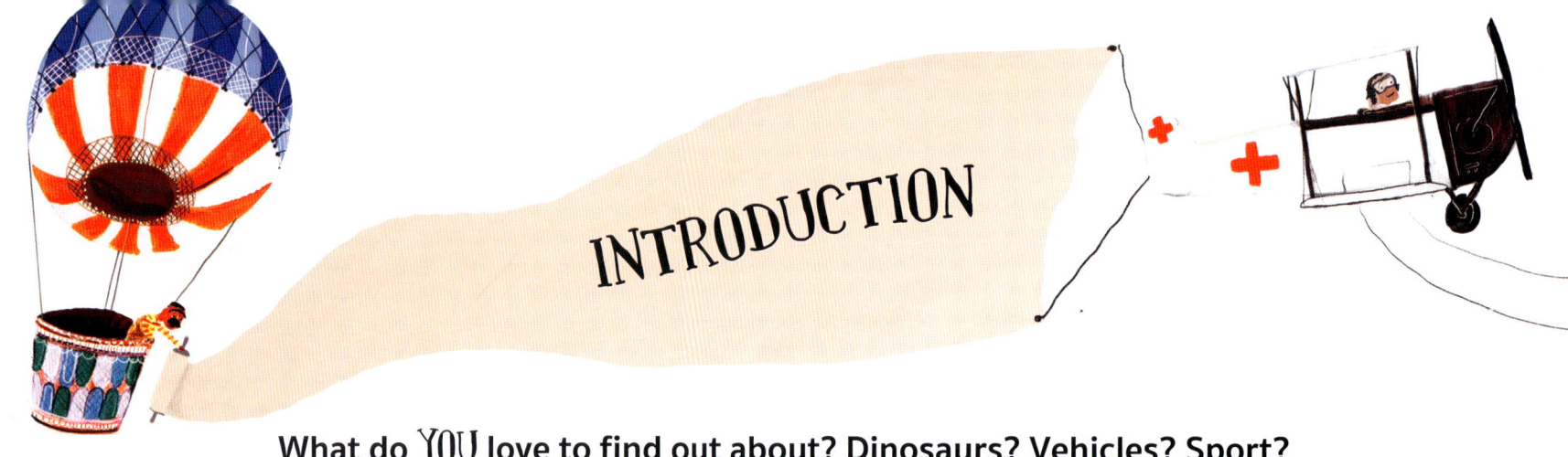

What do YOU love to find out about? Dinosaurs? Vehicles? Sport? Is it amazing animals and their habitats, or incredible inventions that changed the world? The games people have played for fun, or the brilliant buildings they have designed?

In this book you'll find all of these and more . . . but instead of zooming IN to find out about just one thing at a time, we'll be zooming OUT and looking at the world as one enormous timeline of EVERYTHING. Along the way, you'll find the surprising answers to all sorts of questions – such as . . .

Did people pay with paper money or coins first?

What are the oldest sweets? (Yum!)

Are forks older than chopsticks?

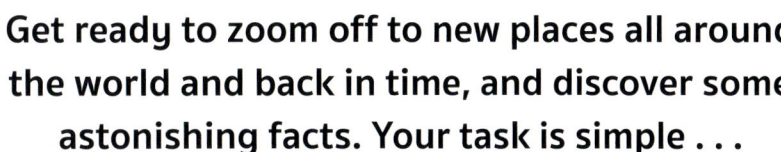

Get ready to zoom off to new places all around the world and back in time, and discover some astonishing facts. Your task is simple . . .

- Find the questions on each page.
- Guess what came first for each one.
- Once you've had a go, read on to see if you guessed correctly.
- Use the mind-boggling facts you've found to impress your teachers, family and friends!

Let's warm up with a quick 'what came first' question.

ICE SKATES OR ROLLER SKATES?

People have been whizzing around on skates for a long time, but wrap up warm . . . the first ones were ice skates!

When lakes or rivers froze in cold places, ice skates were a useful shortcut – some from northern Europe date to around 3000BCE. Roller skates were born much later, in the Netherlands in the early 1700s. They allowed keen ice skaters to carry on even when there was no ice. There was one drawback to early roller skates, though . . . their design made turning corners difficult!

READY FOR MORE? TURN THE PAGE!

SNAKES AND LADDERS OR NOUGHTS AND CROSSES?

If you went for three in a row, you're the winner! Noughts and crosses (or tic-tac-toe) is older.

Noughts and crosses

Ancient Egyptians loved to play noughts and crosses, where players try to make a row of three. A version of this game has been found on Egyptian roof tiles dating to 1300 BCE.

Ancient Romans had a similar game called *terni lapilli*, where players would try to get pebbles or other counters in a row. Try this yourself if you don't have pencils and paper to hand!

Tech-tac-toe
An early video game called OXO was based on noughts and crosses. It was created in 1952 by British computer scientist Alexander S Douglas.

Snakes and ladders

This game was invented in India – the earliest boards found so far are from the 1700s. Religious teachers used it to teach about karma (the belief that people are rewarded or punished for their actions). Ladders represented good actions; snakes represented bad ones. Some boards had more snakes than ladders, so reaching the end of the game could be hard work!

TELEVISION OR CINEMA?

In Paris, France in December 1895, a long queue formed . . . it was for the first commercial cinema screening! French inventors Auguste and Louis Lumière had made a machine for projecting moving images. Television came later – the first public demonstration was in January 1926 in London, by Scottish engineer John Logie Baird.

BOOKS OR NEWSPAPERS?

Okay, it depends on how you define a book... but written stories didn't always look like the object you're holding! The oldest 'books' are much older than newspapers.

Books

The earliest written stories we know about were made in ancient Mesopotamia (an area around modern-day Iraq). They were carved on clay tablets – one, called the *Epic of Gilgamesh*, was made around 2000 BCE.

And what about printed books? The oldest one found so far is a copy of a Buddhist religious text called the *Diamond Sutra* from around 868 CE. The words and images were carved on wood then painted with ink, ready to be transferred onto paper. If you've ever tried using a stamp, you've made something similar!

Newspapers

In the early 1450s, German goldsmith Johannes Gutenberg invented a printing press with movable type. This clever invention had metal letters covered in ink that were pressed onto paper. It made printing identical sheets much easier – including the first newspapers! The oldest is thought to be a German one called *Relation*, from 1605.

Hear all about it!

When early newspapers started being printed, many people couldn't read. Many people in the UK relied on a town crier – someone who would walk around ringing a bell and shouting about important events.

SWEETS OR CHOCOLATE BARS?

Humans have been enjoying both for thousands of years – but it was sweets that came first! Chocolate bars came later than you might think . . .

Sweets

What comes to mind when you think of sweets? Some of the first ones we know about used honey. One ancient Egyptian recipe from around 1600BCE includes ground-up dates, chopped walnuts and cinnamon, which are formed into balls then rolled in honey and ground almonds. Gobstoppers of the ancient world!

Chocolate bars

Chocolate is made from the beans of the cacao tree. Civilisations in Mexico and Central and South America began using cacao thousands of years ago – around 3300BCE for the South American Mayo-Chinchipe people. In the 1600s, chocolate blocks were brought to Europe, but sugary chocolate bars came later. In 1847, a company called Fry's mixed cocoa powder and butter with sugar, moulded it . . . and made modern chocolate bars!

Chocolatey drinks

From around 1800BCE, the Mayans (a Central America civilisation) made cacao drinks. They were often made with maize (corn). Some were sweetened with honey or flowers. Others were spiced with chilli!

BIRTHDAY PRESENTS OR BIRTHDAY CAKE?

It's hard to tell which came first as both are ancient – but it was probably presents!

Presents

Around 3000 BCE, ancient Egyptian pharaohs started having big coronation celebrations. Egyptians thought that when pharaohs were crowned, they became gods. It was a birthday party for their new life! Pharaohs often received gifts, much like birthday presents today.

Cake

The ancient Greeks loved a celebration – and cake! From around the 5th century BCE, they held the springtime Mounichia festival to honour the goddess Artemis. As part of the celebration, cakes ringed with small torches were offered. This may be where the idea of birthday cake candles came from!

CROCODILES OR TRICERATOPS?

You might think that dinosaurs came before animals that are alive today – but crocodiles are older than lots of dinosaurs, including Triceratops!

Crocodiles

Ahh, a lovely calm river . . . a balmy evening . . . the perfect conditions for a dip – just watch out for crocodiles! These huge predators were hunting their prey long before people walked the Earth. Early crocodile ancestors were called Protosuchia and lived in the late Triassic period (237–201 million years ago). It was around this time that the first dinosaurs started emerging.

Crocodiles might look like living dinosaurs, but they have changed a lot over time. Some ancient crocodiles were herbivores (plant-eaters)!

Distant cousins
What do a pigeon and a crocodile have in common? More than you might think. Crocodiles and birds are each other's closest living relatives.

Ancient animals
Other animals older than Triceratops include lobsters, duck-billed platypuses and cockroaches!

Triceratops

Snuffle . . . snort . . . what's that sound? It's Triceratops, hunting for delicious palm fronds! These impressive dinosaurs lived in the late Cretaceous period (101–66 million years ago). They shared their world with predators such as Tyrannosaurus, so they needed to be careful. One Triceratops fossil has a horn with signs of healing after being bitten, showing that some survived attacks.

PET CATS OR PET DOGS?

Are you a cat person or a dog person? If you're on team dog, you've won this one! Dogs were domesticated long before cats started curling up in our houses.

Dogs

People likely started keeping dogs as pets around 14,000–30,000 years ago. Dogs are descended from wolves but there are different theories on how they first bonded with people. Some researchers think that wolves started following humans and eating their leftovers – and the relationship grew from there!

Cats

People and cats have been spending time together for around 10,000–12,000 years. When humans began farming in the Middle East, they needed to store their grain. Pests like mice were a problem . . . but cats came to the rescue! These pests were an easy snack for cats who gathered near human settlements, and eventually they became domesticated. A good deal!

Cat gods

The ancient Egyptians worshipped cats. The goddess Bastet was often shown with a cat's head, and mummifying cats was common. One ancient Egyptian cemetery contained 300,000 cat mummies!

BUSES OR STEAM TRAINS?

If you said buses, well done! The first bus that carried passengers along a fixed route was around 140 years before the first steam train began puffing along its track.

Buses

Picture yourself in Paris in 1662. The River Seine is rushing under bridges, and the first bus has passengers boarding! These horse-drawn carriages could carry 6–8 people but weren't on the roads for long. They were only available for wealthy upper-class people who didn't need them, so they stopped operating by 1675. Fast forward to the 1800s, though, and buses were back, in Paris and other cities such as London – around the same time as steam trains! Buses were still expensive at first. In the 1890s, electric trams became a more affordable option.

Steam trains

The first steam train, built in 1804, transported iron rather than people. It was built by English engineer Robert Trevithick to take metal from Penydarren, south Wales, to a canal just over 15 kilometres to the south. A local businessman bet 500 guineas that it couldn't be done – over £43,000 in today's money!

Passengers on board

The first steam train to transport passengers and goods was the Stockton and Darlington railway in northern England. It steamed away on 27 September 1825, carrying 450 passengers. It travelled at 24 kilometres per hour – today, some trains can travel at over 350 kilometres per hour!

AMBULANCE SERVICE OR FIRE SERVICE?

Emergency medicine and firefighting have been organised in lots of different ways – but when it comes to a dedicated city service, firefighting came first!

Fire service

Before the invention of machines, firefighting usually involved pumping water into buckets by hand – hard, slow work! The first city fire service was created in 1824 by firefighter James Braidwood, in Edinburgh, Scotland. It wasn't long before it was needed – a large, destructive fire broke out in the city the same year.

The first air ambulance – the Flying Doctor – launched in Australia in 1928. This was a quick way to help people in rural areas. It is still running today!

Ambulance service

Early ambulances were horse-drawn wagons on battlefields – but the first city ambulance service run from a hospital was in Cincinnati, Ohio, US. This horse-drawn service began in 1865 – other places, such as New York City in the US, followed shortly after.

WINDSCREEN WIPERS OR SEAT BELTS?

It was seat belts! English inventor George Cayley designed an early seat belt in the 1800s, to keep him secure in his glider. American inventor Mary Anderson created windscreen wipers in 1903 after noticing a tram driver getting out to wipe snow from the window. In 1959, the three-point car seat belts we use today were invented by Swedish engineer Nils Bohlin.

DIVING BOARDS OR WATER SLIDES?

Have you ever jumped off a diving board, or whooshed down a water slide? Both can give a thrilling rush of adrenaline – but it was diving boards that came first!

Diving for gold

Diving became an Olympic sport in 1904. Synchronised diving (where two people perform an identical dive) was added to the programme in 2000.

Diving boards

Though people have been diving for thousands of years, the first records come from ancient Greece. Some vases and paintings from the 5th and 6th centuries BCE have decorations of people diving off cliffs!

Modern diving, where athletes perform different flips and twists, became popular in the 19th century. The first diving association was founded in Halle, Germany in 1840. The group gained the nickname 'Tichy's frogs', after one of the founding divers, named Tichy.

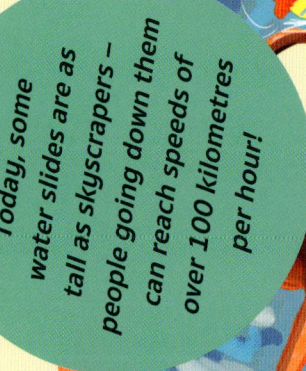

Today, some water slides are as tall as skyscrapers – people going down them can reach speeds of over 100 kilometres per hour!

Water slides

The first account of a water slide is from Christchurch, New Zealand in 1906. Visitors could sit in wooden 'chute boats' that slid down a track and into nearby Victoria Lake. Even the city's governor, Lord Plunket, had a go. He was usually quite serious . . . but a local newspaper reported that he came out of the slide with a massive grin on his face!

SWIMMING POOLS OR TRAMPOLINES?

SPLASH! If you guessed swimming pools, well done – when it comes to sports, swimming pools came first.

Swimming pools

The ancient Greeks REALLY loved their sports. In 776BCE they created the first Olympic games – talented athletes were given big prizes and lots of praise! Some ancient Greek gyms, called *palastrae*, included pools. Athletes would probably have used these to warm up or cool down their muscles during training – some of the pools would have had freezing water!

Trampolines

Sports trampolines were developed in the 1940s. On a trip to the circus, American gymnast George Nissen watched performers dropping onto safety nets. He saw them bounce slightly when they landed . . . and an idea formed in his mind. It inspired him to make a 'tumbling device' – an early trampoline!

Some astronauts used a trampolining game called spaceball to train for zero gravity conditions. Two astronauts would bounce on a three-sided trampoline while throwing a ball to each other.

SPECTACLES OR SUNGLASSES?

It's a bit complicated! Sunglasses with special protective lenses emerged after early spectacles . . . but sun protection goggles are thousands of years old!

Sunglasses

Sunlight and snow can be a dangerous combination. Too much exposure can cause snow blindness – a bit like sunburn, but in the eyes. Around 2,000 years ago, in the far north of North America, Inuits developed protective goggles for days spent out in the bright snowy landscape. They were made of bone, wood or ivory and had a slit in the middle to see through. Sunglasses with protective lenses to filter out harmful UV light weren't available until the 1900s.

Centuries ago in China, dark glasses were used for rituals and ceremonies – they were often made from smoky quartz, a gemstone with a brownish tint.

Spectacles

Around 1000, people started using glass or crystal 'reading stones' to make text easier to read – but it wasn't until the 1200s that these aids were used over eyes. Many early spectacles had to be held in place by hand – but in 1727, English optician Edward Scarlett invented 'sides' to hold spectacles on the face. Now, they could be worn all day!

HAIR GEL OR HAIR DRYERS?

It was hair gel! Some ancient Egyptian mummies from around 2,300–3,500 years ago have been found with perfumed animal fat in their wigs, likely used for styling. The first hair dryer was invented in 1888 by French hair salon owner Alexandre Ferdinand Godefroy. His large, helmet-like machine was inspired by the vacuum cleaner!

PROSTHETICS OR HEARING AIDS?

If you guessed prosthetics, you are right. These artificial body parts have been in use for around 3,000 years.

Prosthetics

Some of the earliest prosthetics we know about are ancient Egyptian big toes. One, made of wood and designed for the right foot, was found in a tomb dating from 1065–740 BCE. Another ancient Egyptian toe was made from a papier-mâché-like mix including linen and glue. Prosthetic legs were also made in ancient Rome and China around 300 BCE.

An artificial eye from around 2800 BCE was found in the ancient city of Shahr-i Sokhta, in modern-day Iran. It belonged to a young woman.

Hearing aids

Today, hearing aids fit neatly inside the ear – but early ones were MUCH bigger. They were named hearing trumpets, as they looked a little like musical trumpets, and had to be held up to the ear. The first writing about these devices was in 1634, by French priest and mathematician Jean Leurechon.

PARTY BALLOONS OR HOT AIR BALLOONS?

Hot air balloons came first! These huge inventions were the first way that humans took to the skies. Let's head up into the clouds to find out more – hold on tight . . .

Hot air balloons

In 1783 in a small town in the south of France, two brothers named Joseph-Michel and Jacques-Étienne Montgolfier discovered that putting hot air in a paper bag caused the bag to rise up – and the idea for the hot air balloon was born.

In September 1783, they launched the first balloon flight with passengers . . . a sheep, a rooster and a duck! The animals landed safely about eight minutes later. The stage was set for the first balloon flight with human passengers in November 1783, above Paris, France.

DIY balloons

Inventor Thomas Hancock began selling a balloon kit in 1825 – this included a rubber mixture for people to make their own balloons!

Party balloons

We have British physicist and chemist Michael Faraday to thank for these classic party decorations. He created the balloon in 1824 by putting two sheets of rubber together with a layer of flour inbetween to stop them sticking, then pumping hydrogen between the sheets. Hydrogen is lighter than air . . . so up floated the first balloon!

BASKETBALL OR TABLE TENNIS?

Both of these games – now Olympic sports – emerged in the last 150 years, but it was table tennis that came first!

Table tennis

This tabletop sport was invented in England in the 1880s as an after-dinner game. At first, players used whatever equipment they could find, such as books for a net. The sport became popular and the first European championships were held in 1926. Table tennis was also part of the original line up of eight sports at the first Paralympic Games in Rome in 1960.

Table tennis is very popular today. There are around 40 million competitive players in the world, plus likely millions more who play for fun.

Basketball

Canadian-American educator James Naismith invented this much-loved sport in 1891 in Massachusetts, US, as a way to keep his students active in the winter. The name comes from the original goals – two peach baskets. In early games, the baskets didn't have a hole in the bottom. If a goal was scored, someone needed to go up a stepladder to retrieve the ball!

Changing rules

James Naismith kept tweaking and adapting the rules of basketball into what are now known as the original 13 rules.

PAPER MONEY OR COINS?

Coins and notes have come in useful for centuries as an exact way of paying for things, but it was coins that came first.

Coins

Metal has been used as money for a long time, but early metal money did not have any standard weights or exact values. Around 600BCE, King Alyattes of Lydia, in modern-day Turkey, came up with a way to make things simpler. He introduced tokens that weighed the same, stamped with the royal symbol of a lion – the first coins were in circulation!

As well as coins and paper, other objects have been used as money, such as shells, whale teeth and pieces of leather.

Paper money

Paper was invented in China – and so were the first paper notes! Paper money was much lighter than coins. It was first used in the 700s. Merchants would deposit money with trusted officials in exchange for a paper receipt, that could be swapped for money in different places. In the Song dynasty (960–1279), people started using paper notes as currency, like notes today (using the notes to pay for things rather than just swapping them for money).

CLOCKS OR COMPASSES?

People have been using both of these clever instruments for many years – but it was the clock that came first.

Clocks
The earliest clocks were sundials, created by the ancient Egyptians around 1500BCE – possibly earlier. These clocks used the movement of the sun to cast shadows that moved around a piece of stone, a bit like hands on a clock face. Another ancient type of clock used in ancient civilisations was a *clepsydra*, or water clock. This worked like an hourglass, but with water instead of sand.

Compasses
Compasses work because of a force called magnetism that pulls towards the north. Certain rocks, such as lodestone, are naturally magnetic. People have known about magnetism for thousands of years – ancient Greeks knew that lodestone could attract iron. However, it wasn't until the 1100s that people started using compasses for navigation at sea.

Magnet magic

The area that a magnet affects is called its magnetic field – there's one stretching all the way around Earth.

FORKS OR CHOPSTICKS?

It was chopsticks! They were first used as a way of getting food out of cooking pots, but became common as eating tools in eastern Asia around 400CE. People began using forks for eating around 600CE. Greek noblewoman Maria Argyropoulina used a golden fork at her wedding in Venice in 1004. This was a surprising choice at the time – most people at the event were used to eating with their fingers!

SCHOOLS OR LIBRARIES?

Pens and pencils at the ready... schools came first!

Schools

Schools have been around since the start of written history around 3000BCE. Many ancient civilisations had their own schools – though they could be very different. In ancient Egypt, they were often for training priests and scribes. Ancient Chinese schools focused on morals, and duty to others and the state.

Ancient PE lessons

Lots of civilisations have taught PE over time. In Sparta (a city-state in ancient Greece), children had lessons in wrestling!

Libraries

Gathering amazing writing is an ancient idea – an early library, in Ebla in modern-day Syria, was created around 2500–2350BCE. But what about libraries with an organised filing system? The prize for this goes to the Royal Library of Ashurbanipal in Nineveh, an ancient city located in modern-day Iraq. King Ashurbanipal was a tough warrior – and a book lover. His library, created between 668–631BCE, held around 30,000 texts in many different languages.

SIGN LANGUAGE OR BRAILLE?

Did you guess sign language? You're correct!

Sign language

Many different people have used signs to communicate over time. Ancient Greek philosopher Plato wrote about people using sign language around 380 BCE. In the 10th century, monks at Cluny Abbey in France pioneered sign language to communicate, as many had taken vows of silence.

In 19th century North America, indigenous people from the Great Plains who spoke different languages communicated with signs – such as a circle drawn in the air for the Moon.

Braille

Braille is a written system of raised dots that blind or visually impaired people touch to read. It was created by French educator Louis Braille in 1824. Blind since childhood, Braille noticed that reading systems for blind people were hard to learn . . . so he made a better option, at the age of 15!

HIGH FIVES OR HANDSHAKES?

It was handshakes! They are at least 3,000 years old. Artwork from the 800s BCE shows the kings of Assyria and Babylon shaking hands. The high five likely evolved from the low five in the 1900s. In an iconic moment at a 1977 baseball game, teammates Dusty Baker and Glenn Burke high fived to celebrate a home run!

THE TAJ MAHAL OR THE GREAT WALL OF CHINA?

Both of these jaw-dropping feats of engineering are still standing – but the Great Wall of China came first.

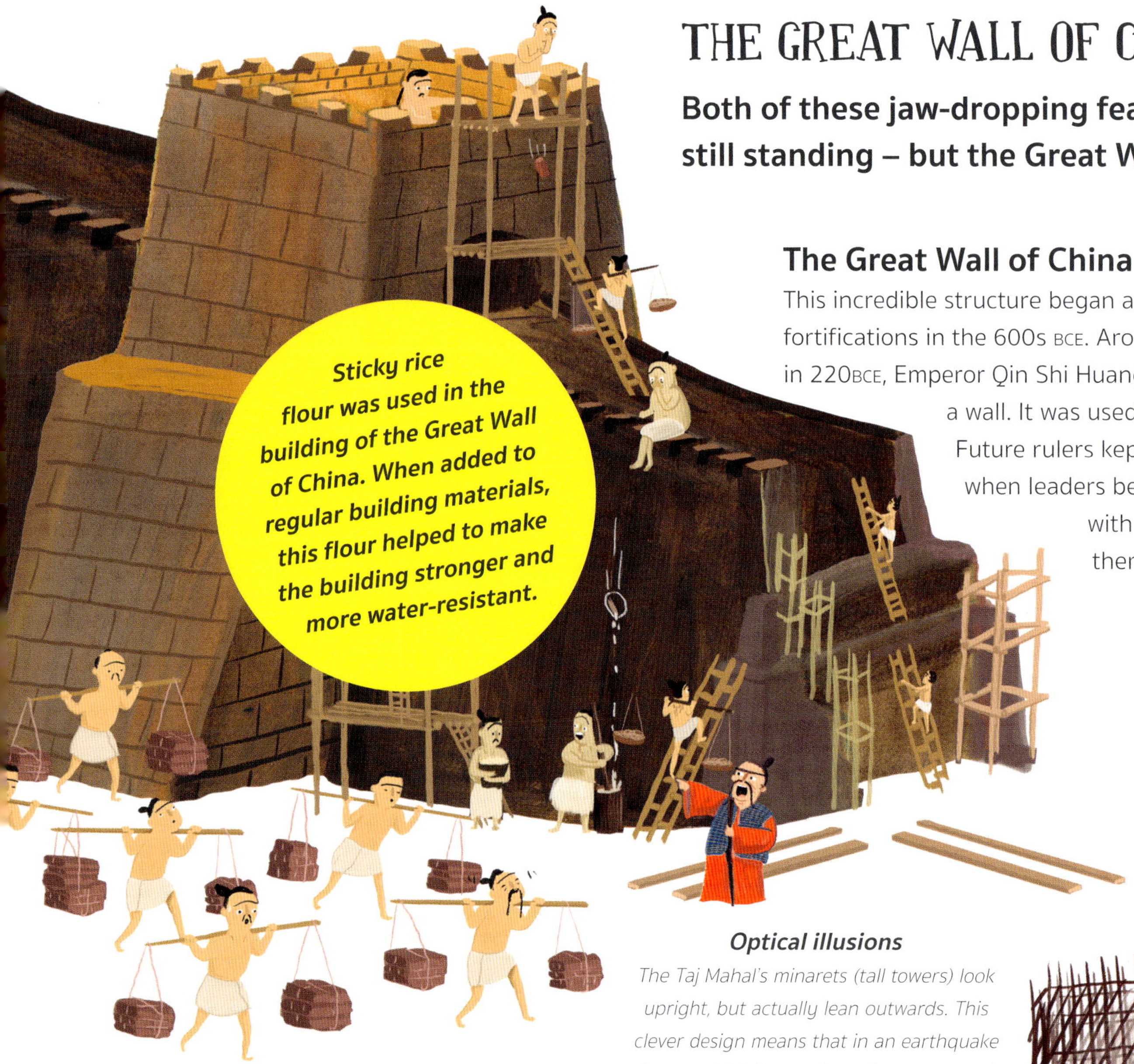

The Great Wall of China

This incredible structure began as a series of ancient fortifications in the 600s BCE. Around 400 years later in 220 BCE, Emperor Qin Shi Huang began connecting these into a wall. It was used as protection from invasions. Future rulers kept working on it until the 1600s, when leaders began more peaceful negotiating with their neighbours. This meant there was less need for the wall.

Sticky rice flour was used in the building of the Great Wall of China. When added to regular building materials, this flour helped to make the building stronger and more water-resistant.

Optical illusions
The Taj Mahal's minarets (tall towers) look upright, but actually lean outwards. This clever design means that in an earthquake they would fall away from the monument.

The Taj Mahal

Emperor Shah Jahan built this spectacular building between 1632–1643 as a momument to his wife, Mumtaz Mahal, after she died. A huge amount of material was needed – it took 1,000 elephants to transport it all to the site! Many specialists worked on different parts of the building, such as carving the marble.

MACHU PICCHU OR STONEHENGE?

Let's journey back to south-western England in the late Neolithic age . . . yes, Stonehenge came first!

Stonehenge

This circle of enormous stones was built between 3000–1500BCE. It's a bit of a mystery what it was used for. Some archaeologists think it might have been a monument to celebrate people's links with their ancestors. Others think it may have been a temple to the Sun and Moon. Another mystery is how the stones were moved. Many were brought from over 200 kilometres away!

Modern celebrations
Stonehenge is positioned to align with the Sun at the solstice, when the Sun is at its highest point in the sky. Each year, around 20,000 people gather to watch and celebrate together.

Machu Picchu

Machu Picchu is a ruined settlement in the Andes mountains in Peru, originally built by the Inca, a South American civilisation. It was built in the first half of the 1400s as a summer retreat, with areas for farming and houses carefully built into the mountain location. The Inca didn't make written records, but archaeologists can study objects and buildings to learn more about how people in Machu Picchu lived.

TIMELINE

You've finished all the questions, hooray! How many did you guess correctly?

Explore this timeline to see some of the amazing events and discoveries covered in this book. The early years are approximate.

1662 First horse-drawn bus journey

1783 First hot air balloon flight

1804 First steam train built

1824 First city fire service / First rubber balloon invented / Braille invented

1847 Fry's made the first chocolate bars

1865 First city ambulance service

1632–43 The Taj Mahal built

1605 An early newspaper, *Relation*, printed

1450s Gutenberg printing press invented

1400s Machu Picchu built

1100s Compasses first used for navigation at sea

868 CE The first printed book, a copy of the *Diamond Sutra*, is created

237–201 million years ago Early crocodile ancestors lived

101–66 million years ago Triceratops lived

28000–12000 BCE* Dogs domesticated

10000–8000 BCE Cats domesticated

3300 BCE Mayo-Chinchipe people began using cacao

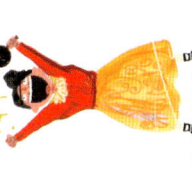

3000–1500 BCE
Stonehenge built

1800 BCE
Mayans began making chocolate drinks

1600 BCE
Ancient Egyptians made date and honey sweets

1500 BCE
Ancient Egyptian sundials created

800s BCE
Handshake shown in carving

700s CE
Paper money first used

380 BCE
Plato wrote about sign language

600s–500s BCE
Divers shown in ancient Greek art

600s BCE
Great Wall of China early structures built
First standardised coins

1880s
Table tennis invented

1891
Basketball invented

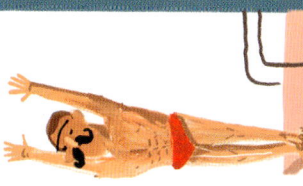

1895
First commercial cinema screening

1900s
First high fives

1903
Windscreen wipers invented

1906
First account of a water slide

1926
First TV demonstration

1959
Three-point car seat belts invented

*BCE means Before the Common Era (the birth of Jesus Christ). CE means after the Common Era.

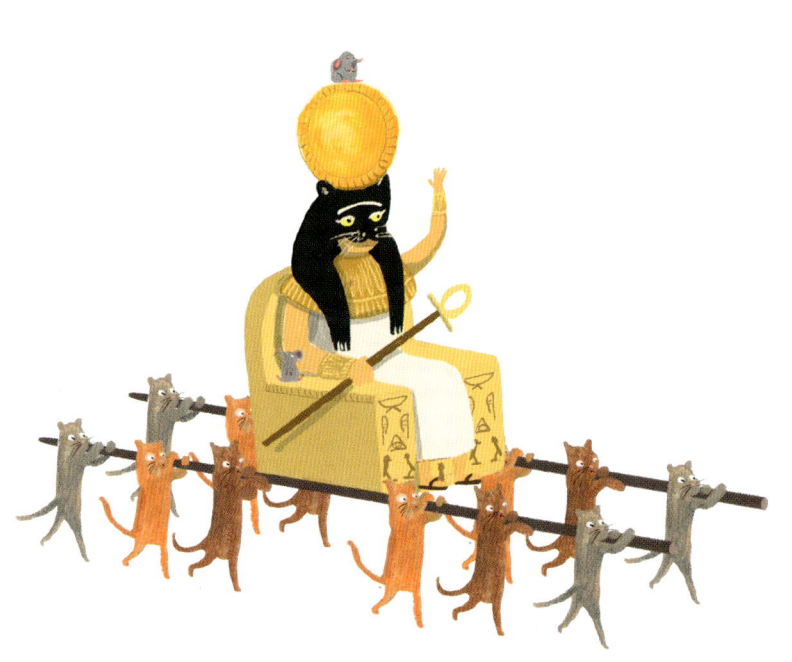